Written by Jennifer Jordan
Illustrated by Ken Morton

ISBN 0 86112 773 0

Printed in Hong Kong for Chad Valley Books,
242–246 Marylebone Road, London, NW1 6JL.

The Adventures of
Silly Tilly Witch
and her Friends

CHAD VALLEY

SPOOKY the TEAPOT GHOST

Spooky the ghost lived in a big
blue teapot in a garden shed.
It was an old dusty teapot.
It had no lid and a funny spout.
But Spooky liked his cosy home.
No-one knew he lived there.
He could fly around all day
and no-one could see him.

But Spooky had no friends.
"No-one knows who I am," he said.
"No-one can see a ghost."
He went to the park and fed the ducks.
He sat on the swings
and slid down the slide.
Then he threw a ball for a dog.
But no-one spoke to him.
No-one knew he was there.

One day he flew out of his teapot.
He flew over the town and over the fields
He sat in a tree in Dapple Wood.
It was sports day and all the animals were having fun.
''Maybe I can have some fun too,'' said Spooky. ''No-one can see me, so I can play some tricks.''

First it was the running race.
The animals stood in a line
waiting for the race to begin.
''Ready . . . Steady . . . Go!''
All the animals fell over.
''Who said that?'' asked Miffy Mouse.
They looked all around them
but no-one could see Spooky
in the tree.

Then it was the high jump.
Miffy Mouse fixed a long pole
between two trees.
But Spooky moved the pole.
He moved it far too high
and no-one could jump over it.
"Who moved the pole?"
asked Miffy Mouse.
They looked up in the trees.
But no-one could see Spooky the ghost.

The sack race was next.
But Spooky moved the finishing post in to the middle of Dapple Stream!
All the animals were very wet and very cross.
''Someone is playing tricks on us,'' said Miffy Mouse. But no-one could see Spooky. He waved goodbye as he flew home to his big blue teapot.

That night Oscar Owl tapped on the window of the garden shed.
''You played those tricks, Spooky,'' he said. ''I know it was you.''
Spooky peeped out of his teapot.
''I am a ghost,'' said Spooky.
''You cannot see me.''
''I cannot see you in the daytime,'' said Oscar. ''But you glow in the dark, so I can see you now!''

Oscar Owl was very kind. Spooky said he was sorry for playing tricks.
"Then come to Dapple Wood with me," said Oscar. They flew off into the dark sky.
"I have never been out in the dark before," said Spooky. "Look, I really am glowing!"
The streets and fields lit up as Spooky flew by.

The animals in Dapple Wood
were wide awake.
Spooky and Oscar flew down
beside them, Spooky saw that
the animals looked sad.
''What is the matter?'' he asked.
''We cannot leave the wood,''
said Mr Mole.
''We would get lost in the dark,''
said Boris Badger.
''So we never have any fun,''
said Rosie Rabbit.

''Come with me,'' said Spooky.
He led the animals to the garden shed.
''I have never been out of the wood before,'' said Rosie Rabbit.
''We cannot get lost,'' said Mr Mole.
''Spooky is glowing like a torch.''
''We will take my teapot back to Dapple Wood,'' said Spooky.
''Then we can have some fun.''
The animals pushed and pulled the teapot back to Dapple Wood.
They were all puffing.
''This is not fun,'' said Boris Badger.

Back in Dapple Wood they pushed
the teapot into Dapple Stream.
''All aboard!'' said Spooky.
But as the animals climbed onto
the teapot, it began to wobble.
''Help!'' called Mr Mole. ''I am
going to fall!''
Splash! Mr Mole fell in to Dapple Stream.
Boris Badger and Rosie Rabbit
pulled him out.
''Now I am all wet,'' said Mr Mole.
''Never mind,'' said Spooky. ''Now we
are going on an adventure!''

They sailed down the stream to the river.
Very soon they were sailing on the sea.
They sailed up and down on the waves.
The big blue teapot landed on a beach.
Spooky and the animals played on
the sand and looked for seashells.
"This is such fun!" said Rosie Rabbit.

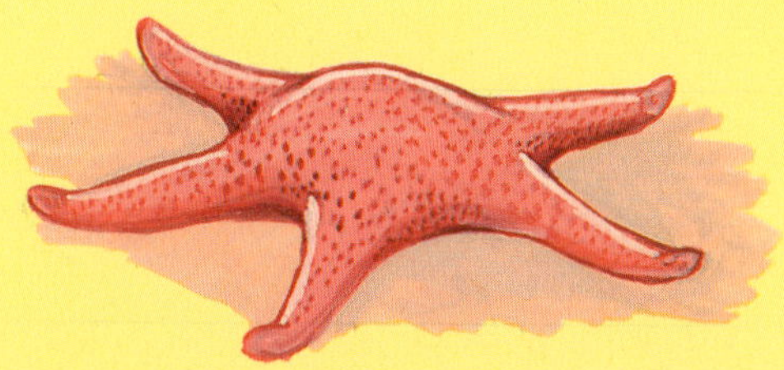

The next morning they sailed home.
The big blue teapot was warm and dry in a tree trunk. Spooky slept all day.
Every night he stayed awake with his new friends.
They had such fun sailing away in the big blue teapot.
"It is nice being a ghost after all," said Spooky.

Say these words again.

cosy
tricks
running
sack
waved
window
playing

glowing
streets
wood
torch
puffing
garden
sailing

What can you see?

teapot

seashells

ducks

shed

trunk

SIZZLE
the
GRUMPY DRAGON

Sizzle the Dragon had a bad cold. His nose was red and he sneezed all day long. He tried to blow fire from his nose. But he could only huff and puff.
''You have a cold,'' said his friends. ''You will blow fire when you are better.''
But Sizzle sat on a log and felt very grumpy.

''You can have my blue scarf to keep you warm,'' said Dinky Dog.
''And my red scarf,'' said Holly Hare.
''And my yellow scarf,'' said Fluffy Cat.
Buzzy Bee gave him some honey.
Nutty Squirrel gave him some acorn tea. But Sizzle was still a very grumpy dragon.

''We must cheer Sizzle up,''
said Dinky Dog.
Every day they told him funny jokes. Holly Hare stood on her head and sang songs. Fluffy Cat ran after her own tail. Buzzy Bee flew past upside down.
But Sizzle did not smile.
''I have a bad cold,'' he said.
''I feel very grumpy.''

Then Dinky Dog juggled balls in the air. He dropped two and three hit him on the head. Sizzle still did not smile. Then Nutty Squirrel wore a silly hat and made a funny face. But Sizzle was still grumpy.
His friends went away and left him on his own.

The next day Sizzle woke up early.
''Do you know what day it is today, Fluffy Cat?'' asked Sizzle.
''It is Friday,'' said Fluffy Cat.
''Do you know what day it is today, Buzzy Bee?'' asked Sizzle.
''Yes, it is Friday,'' said Buzzy Bee.
Sizzle felt very grumpy again.
No-one knew it was his birthday.

''Please can I have my blue scarf back?'' asked Dinky Dog.
''And my red scarf,'' said Holly Hare.
''And my yellow scarf,'' said Fluffy Cat.
''I am not better yet,'' said Sizzle.
But he did not sniff or sneeze at all. He took off the scarves.
''Now my neck is cold,'' he said.

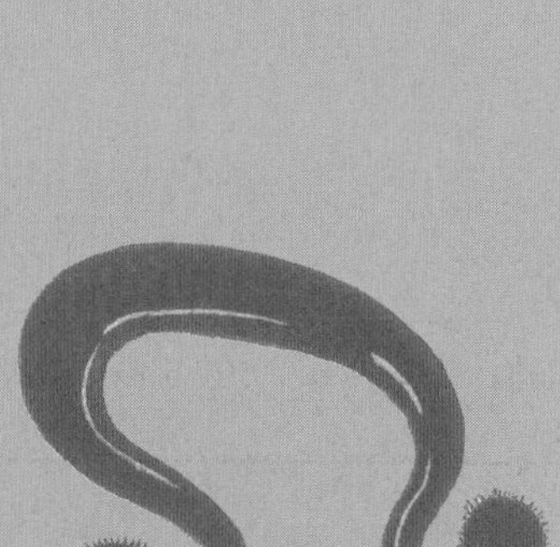

His friends had a lot of work
to do. Sizzle was too grumpy to help,
so he sat under a tree. He saw
Dinky Dog collecting wood.
Then Holly Hare made a big pile
of leaves. Fluffy Cat helped
Nutty Squirrel to carry some boxes.
Buzzy Bee buzzed by with some twigs.
Finally, there was a big pile
of wood and leaves. The animals stood
and looked at their bonfire.

''We cannot light our bonfire,''
said Nutty Squirrel.
Then they saw Sizzle under the tree.
''Please light our bonfire, Sizzle,''
said Dinky Dog.
But Sizzle would not even try.
''I cannot blow fire,'' he said.
''I still have a cold.''

But his friends knew he was better.
So Nutty Squirrel took a pepper pot
and climbed to the top of the tree.
He shook some pepper over Sizzle.
''My nose tickles,'' said Sizzle.
Nutty shook more pepper on to Sizzle.
''Now my nose really tickles,''
said Sizzle.

Then Sizzle gave a very, very big sneeze. A-A-A-TISHOOO!
Fire and smoke blew from his nose.
It blew through the trees
and lit the bonfire.
"Well done, Sizzle," said his friends.
"We knew your cold was better."
But Sizzle was still grumpy.
"It is my birthday," he said.
But no-one heard him.

Then he saw Dinky Dog's blue scarf.
And Holly Hare's red scarf.
And Fluffy Cat's yellow scarf.
They were hanging from the trees.
They had HAPPY BIRTHDAY SIZZLE!
on them, in big letters.
"You knew it was my birthday
all the time!" said Sizzle.

HAPPY
BIRTHDAY
SIZZLE

''We are going to have a party,'' said Buzzy Bee.
They had hot food cooked on the fire. They danced and played games until it was very late. Sizzle had a lot of fun.
''I will never be grumpy again,'' he said. ''From now on I will smile all the time.''

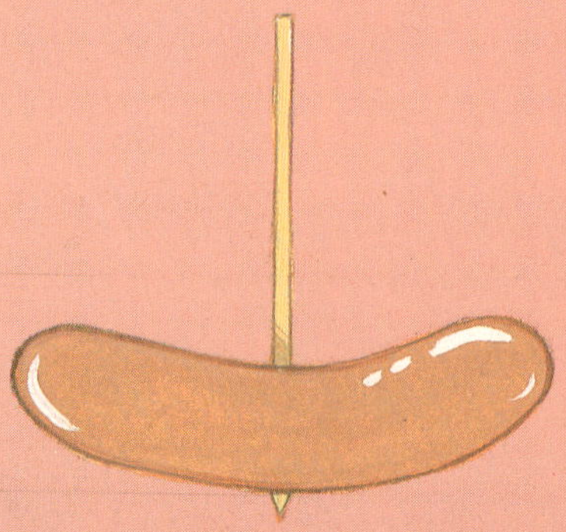

Fluffy Cat made a big birthday cake.
''Now your cold is better, you can light the candles,'' she said.
Sizzle blew fire from his nose and lit all six candles.
''Happy birthday, dear Sizzle, happy birthday to you!'' sang his friends.
Sizzle smiled. He was a very happy dragon indeed!

Say these words again.

grumpy
sneeze
twigs
nose
tickles
candles
yellow

funny
tree
smiled
pepper
honey
jokes
blow

What can you see?

hat

bonfire

birthday cake

leaves

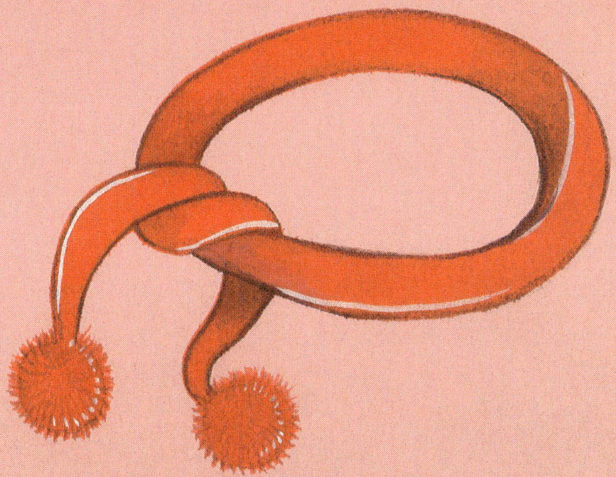

scarf

SILLY TILLY WITCH

Tilly Witch was very cross.
There was a big hole in her roof.
Whenever it rained, water dripped
through all day and all night.
"Drip! Drip! Drip!" she said.
"I am tired of getting wet."
So she wore her big, black hat
to keep dry. She wore it in the bath.
She wore it in bed.
She never, ever took it off.

"I must find my Book of Spells," Tilly said one day. "Then I can magic a new, dry roof." She looked under the bed and under the cat. She looked inside her cooking pot and inside her boots. She shook her broomstick and her thick socks. But she could not find her Book of Spells.

Tilly climbed on to the roof
and sat down. "I cannot mend
this big hole," she said.
"I will try to think of some magic."
She sat very still and said
a magic spell.
"Pink jumping frogs,
a blue spotty mouse.
Please magic a roof,
for my little house."
Then she waited for the spell
to work.

Suddenly the roof began to rock from side to side. Tilly almost fell off. Then it rose up into the air and began to fly. It flew faster and faster. Tilly held on to the chimney pot. "I think that was the wrong spell," she said. "Oh, I am a silly witch!"

Salty Seagull and some of her friends flew by. They were flying home to the sea.
''Our wings are very tired,'' said Salty. ''We have been flying for a long time.''
''Then sit on my roof for a rest,'' said Tilly. They all held on tight as the roof flew on.

Sam and Sally Squirrel ran to the top of a very big hill. They saw the roof flying by and waved their arms.
"Our legs are tired," they said.
"We have been running for a long time."
They jumped on to the roof and sat down for a rest.
"Hold on tight!" said Tilly, as they flew through the sky.

Then they saw Mrs Robin.
Her five babies were flying with her. But they were tired, too.
''Our wings are so small,'' said the baby birds. ''We cannot fly very well.''
''Then come for a ride on my roof,'' said Tilly. ''We can fly very fast.''
There was no more room on the roof as it flew along.

Katy Kitten was sitting on the top of the clock tower. She saw the flying roof go by.
''Help!'' she said. ''I am stuck! I cannot get down!''
Tilly picked up the kitten and went to put her on the roof. But there was no more room to sit down. ''Katy can sit in my pocket,'' said Tilly. ''Now, hold on tight.''

Then the big clock began to chime.
BONG! BONG! BONG! BONG!
''It's four o'clock!'' said Tilly.
''I must get home soon. My house has no roof.''
''But, you're a witch,'' said Sally Squirrel. ''You can magic a new roof.''
''I wish I could,'' said Tilly.
''But I have lost my Book of Spells.''

Suddenly the roof began to wobble.
"The magic has gone," said Tilly.
"We are going to fall off!"
The roof crashed into a big, soft
pile of straw. Everyone fell off.
Then the roof rose into the air and
flew out of sight.
"Oh dear," said Tilly. "Now I have
no roof at all. What am I going to do?"

''We can help,'' said Mrs Robin.
All of Tilly's friends took big piles of straw to Tilly's house. Then the birds began to weave it.
''This is how we make our nests,'' they said. ''And our nests are warm and dry.''
They made a warm, dry roof for Tilly's house.
''Thank you,'' said Tilly.
''How clever.''

Tilly's friends stayed for tea.
It was getting dark when they went home. Tilly felt very tired so she got ready for bed. The new roof had no holes in it.
"I will stay warm and dry all night," she said. "At last I can take off my big, black hat."

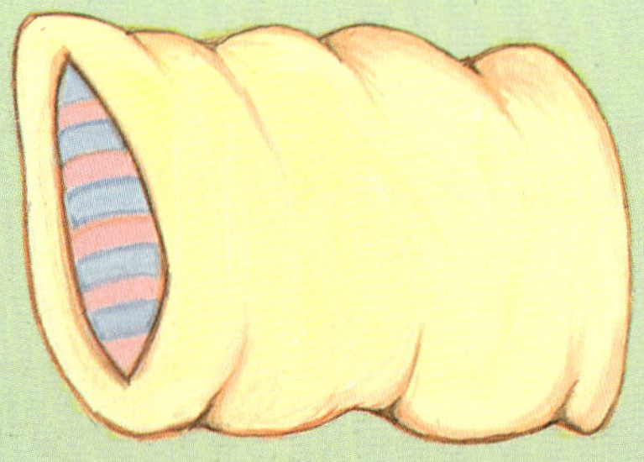

She hung her hat on the door. But as she brushed her hair she began to smile. On top of her head was the lost Book of Spells.

''It was under my hat all the time!'' she said. ''Oh, I am a silly witch.''

Then she put the book under her pillow and fell fast asleep.

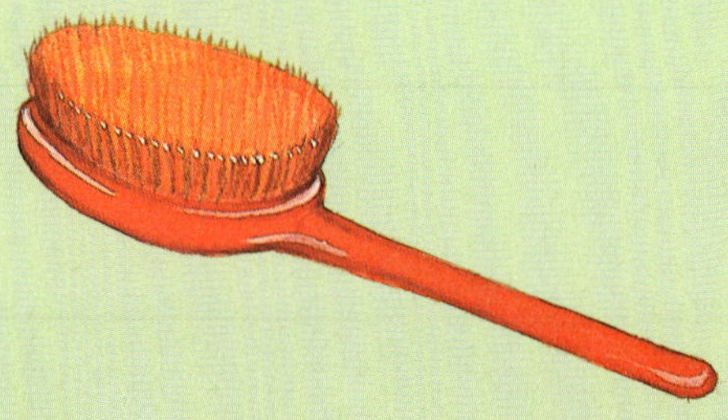

Say these words again.

hole
drip
mend
spell
hill
house
flying

wobble
magic
rests
pocket
weave
clever
warm

What can you see?

roof

hat

broomstick

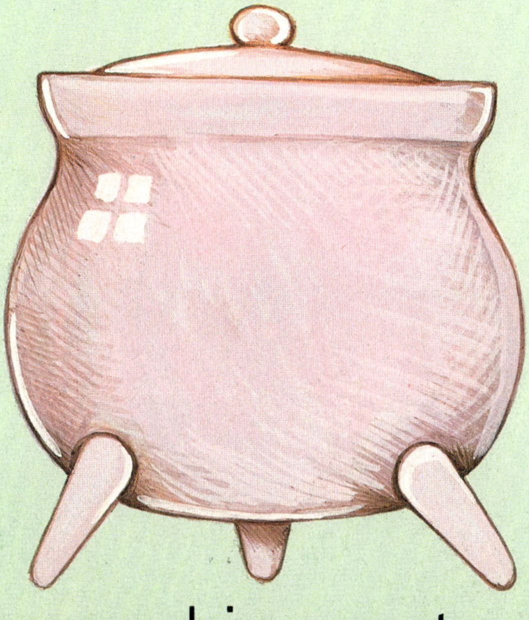

cooking pot

Book of Spells

BIGWIG'S BEDTIME

Bigwig the giant could not sleep.
His feet stuck out of the bed
and his toes were getting very cold.
It was raining and there were no stars
in the sky. It was a very dark
night. Bigwig hid his head under
the sheet. He tried to be brave
but he was afraid of the dark.

The next day Bigwig felt very tired. "I will go for a walk," he said. "The fresh air will wake me up." It was still raining, so he pulled on his big, black boots. He put on his coat and hat to keep him dry and set off for a walk. It was fun to jump and splash in the puddles.

In the town Bigwig saw a very big puddle. It was so big no-one could cross it.
''I can help you cross the puddle,'' said Bigwig.
But the people were afraid of him.
''You are big and brave,'' they said.
''You are never afraid.''
Bigwig did not tell them he was afraid of the dark.

He lifted a truck, a baker's van and a big bus over the puddle. He picked up a train and put it back on the track. ''We will be late for school,'' said the children. So Bigwig turned his big hat upside down to make a boat. The boys and girls sailed across the puddle to school.

But there were still buses, cars, cats and dogs waiting to cross the puddle. So Bigwig bent down on his hands and knees over the water.
''I will be a bridge,'' he said.
They all crossed the puddle on Bigwig's strong back.
''Thank you, Bigwig,'' they said.
No-one was afraid of Bigwig any more.

Soon there were just Farmer Fred and his sheep to cross the puddle. ''We do not like water,'' said the sheep. ''We may fall in.'' So Bigwig picked up the farmer and the sheep. He took a big step over the puddle and a big step over the fields. And Farmer Fred and his sheep were back at the farm.

Farmer Fred had a lot of work to do. He had to plant ten new trees and sweep the yard. And then the sheep needed their woolly coats cut off.

''I can help you plant the trees,'' said Bigwig.

He stuck his thumb in to the ground ten times and made ten big holes for the new trees.

Bigwig watched Farmer Fred's wife as she fed the hens. Suddenly he began to yawn and could not stop.
"Why are you so tired?" asked Farmer Fred's wife.
"I cannot sleep," said Bigwig.
"My feet stick out of bed and my toes get cold.
And I am afraid of the dark."
Farmer Fred and his wife liked Bigwig. So they took him in to a big barn and let him sleep in the hay.

The hay was warm and soft and very soon Bigwig was fast asleep.
But then he began to snore.
What a noise!
The cows woke up. The cats woke up.
The hens woke up. The mice ran across the floor.
Soon Bigwig was snoring so hard he blew the barn door wide open.

He blew away all the dust and dirt in the yard.
''Bigwig has swept the yard for me,'' said Farmer Fred. He went off to cut the sheep's woolly coats. Then Farmer Fred's wife hung out the wet clothes on the washing line. Bigwig was still snoring. He blew all the washing dry in no time at all.

It was some time later when Bigwig woke up. He rubbed his eyes and sat up in the hay.
''Thank you, Bigwig,'' said Farmer Fred. ''You helped us while you were asleep!''
Then Farmer Fred's wife gave Bigwig a big brown parcel to take home.
''Do not open it until you go to bed,'' she said.

Bigwig said goodbye and set off on his long walk home. The sky was blue and the sun shone. The big, deep puddle had almost gone. All the boys and girls in the school bus waved. The baker gave him a big cream cake for tea. And the train tooted as it went by.

PRI 636

That night Bigwig opened his parcel. Inside he found a big pair of bedsocks and a teddy bear. Farmer Fred's wife had made them from the sheep's wool. The socks kept his big feet snug and warm. Bigwig cuddled his teddy bear and he never felt afraid of the dark again!

Say these words again.

sleep
toes
boots
puddle
afraid
late
brave

step
barn
snore
wet
washing
school
train

What can you see?

teddy bear

truck

sheep

cream cake

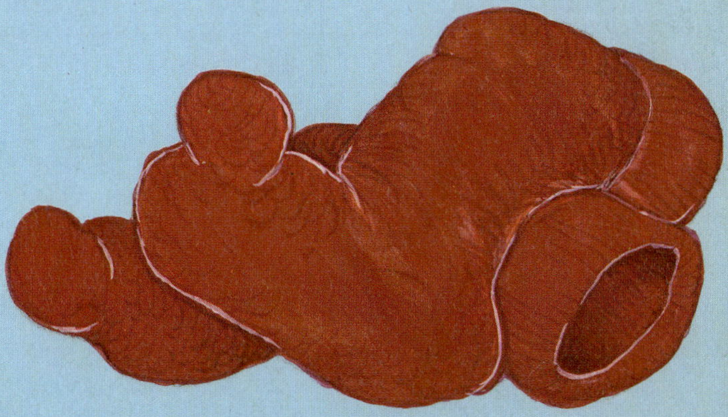

socks